SEE & EXPLORE
LIBRARY

TRAINS
and RAILROADS

Written by
Sydney Wood

Illustrated by
Sergio

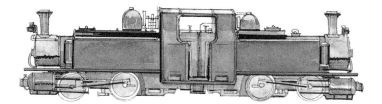

DORLING KINDERSLEY, INC.

NEW YORK

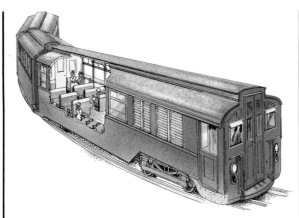

A DORLING KINDERSLEY BOOK

Editors Miranda Smith
Stephen Setford
U.S. editor B. Alison Weir

Senior art editor Chris Scollen

Art director Roger Priddy
Managing editor Ann Kramer

Editorial consultant Julian Holland
Production Shelagh Gibson

First American Edition, 1992

10 9 8 7 6 5 4 3 2 1

Dorling Kindersley, Inc., 232 Madison Avenue
New York, New York 10016

ISBN 1-56458-001-6 (trade)
ISBN 1-56458-002-4 (lib. bdg.)

Library of Congress Catalog Card Number 91-58201

Color Separations by DOT Gradations Limited
Printed in Spain by Artes Graficas: Toledo S. A.
D.L. TO:31-1992

CONTENTS

THE RAILROAD REVOLUTION

Every day, in countries across the globe, hundreds of thousands of people travel by train. Yet 200 years ago, such journeys were impossible. The trains that have opened up new worlds for us ran first in Britain at the beginning of the 19th century. European and North American engineers were quick to adopt the idea of putting steam-powered trains on tracks, and travel by train spread to most

New looks
Railroads have transformed our lives and changed forever the appearance of our towns and cities. In older cities, great spaces have been cleared to make room for the building of stations and the lines that connect them.

A smooth passage
Most modern railroad travel is comfortable for the passengers. Cars travel smoothly along the track, and are well lit and heated. In the last 150 years, engineers have improved the design of engines and cars. Travel by train has become more reliable, safer, and faster.

Under our feet
In many of the world's cities, people plunge underground every day. The trains into which they crowd rush up and down beneath busy streets. Unlike many of the mainline stations, the entrances to underground stations often go unnoticed on the streets. But some stations, such as this one in Moscow, are very impressive inside.

Pulling power
Many kinds of locomotives are used to pull trains. Most trains today use diesel or electric engines, while very few use steam. The trains travel along tracks that slice through hillsides, whiz over bridges, and burrow into mountains, carrying passengers and freight all over the world.

countries in the world. In the 20th century, diesel and electric powered engines have revolutionized railroads, providing efficient high-speed transportation for both people and goods.

The start of a journey
The railroad station, as the gateway to all that railroads had to offer, changed the world. These buildings were so important that sometimes whole new towns grew up around them.

The way in
Train stations are all shapes and sizes. Many have been designed by famous architects and reflect the time and country in which they were built. Some are definitely meant to impress. For example, New York City's Grand Central Station has a 150-foot-high domed ceiling!

Grand Central Station, New York

Melbourne Station, Australia

The Gare de Lyons, Paris

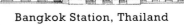

Bangkok Station, Thailand

Down the track
Today's railroads are a vital link between people in different places. Railroads make it possible to travel great distances, enjoy vacations in faraway places, and buy goods made in distant countries.

THE FIRST TRAINS

A Greek inventor called Hero, who lived in Egypt nearly 2,000 years ago, first proved that steam could be used to make objects turn. To entertain people, he made a revolving metal ball that held water and was fixed over a fire. As the water boiled, it turned to steam which escaped through the jets. This spun the ball around.

It was not until the beginning of the 18th century that steam was used successfully to carry out heavy work. The coal and tin mines of the time were being dug deeper, and their products were increasingly in demand, but flooding in mines was a real problem. Steam power was used to work the pumps, which kept the mine shafts free of water.

Engineers also realized that wagons carrying heavy materials such as coal were more easily pulled along rails than along the bumpy roads of the time. These early rails were made of wood and the wagons that ran along them were pulled by horses.

The need for railroads
By the end of the 18th century, improvements in the iron and steel industries resulted in stronger and more reliable steam engines being made. Engineers such as James Watt improved the engines and found ways to power many different types of machines.

The first steam vehicles
James Watt believed it was too dangerous to use steam power to move vehicles; he was afraid of explosion. But his foreman, William Murdoch, was one of the first to build steam-powered cars. In 1769, the Frenchman Nicholas Cugnot amazed crowds in Paris with a machine that managed 2 mph (3 kph) before blowing up. The authorities seized its remains and put Cugnot in prison.

A forceful man
Richard Trevithick was born in 1771, the son of an English tin mine manager. He was very strong and could hurl a sledgehammer over a mine engine house. He was a clever inventor as well as a forceful man. He worked on improving Watt's steam engines and, in 1801, built his first full-size locomotive. This machine ran on the road but ended by crashing into a house.

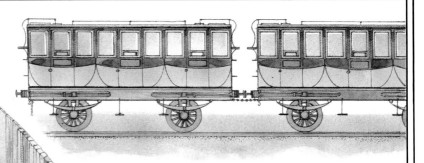

Early coaches

Engineers soon realized that people wished to travel by train. In fact, about 70 people piled onto Trevithick's 1804 bet-winning train. In 1825, the first passenger coach to travel on a railroad - the Stockton and Darlington - was no more than a wooden shed on wheels. These 1838 cars on the Liverpool to Manchester line were made from coach bodies and even had rooftop seats, just like stage coaches.

"Catch Me Who Can"

In 1804, Trevithick won a bet with the owner of an iron works by building a locomotive that pulled a ten-ton load down a 10-mile (16 km) track. In 1808, he built a circular track in London. A high fence surrounded the site so that visitors had to pay a shilling to gaze at the marvel of the locomotive *Catch Me Who Can* steaming around and around. An accident Trevithick could not afford to repair ended the entertainment.

Making tracks

One of the problems that Trevithick faced was finding track strong enough to bear the weight of a steam locomotive. Wooden rails were too weak and, for much of the 18th century, iron rails were too brittle. It was only in the 19th century that rails improved (page 9).

The Newcomen engine

The development of practical working steam engines owed a great deal to an Englishman, Thomas Newcomen. From 1712, he built machines that could pump out water from underground mines. The steam that forced up the piston was rapidly cooled by spraying cold water on the cylinder. This turned the steam back into water and created a vacuum in the space below the piston. The pressure of air outside the cylinder then pushed the piston back down again. The huge crosspiece joining the engine to the pump gave it the name "beam" engine.

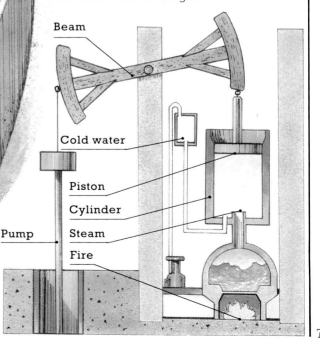

Beam

Cold water

Piston

Cylinder

Pump

Steam

Fire

THE AGE OF STEAM

Despite the work of Richard Trevithick, steam power still seemed too unreliable, too dangerous, and too costly. Also, heavy steam locomotives soon wrecked the wooden track commonly used at the time. Even when iron plates were fastened to the wood, the track was still not strong enough.

The first railroad that regularly carried fare-paying passengers was the Welsh Swansea to Mumbles line of 1806, which used horses. The first North American railroad line opened in 1795, with horses pulling wagons laden with material to build the State House in Boston. When wars between Napoleon's France and other European countries caused the price of horse feed to rise, steam power began to seem attractive. In 1812, the Middleton line at Leeds in England became the first railroad to regularly use steam locomotives. By this time, too, English iron makers had learned how to produce stronger track. William Jessop designed iron rails in sections 2 ft 6 in (75 cm) long with smooth tops along which shaped or flanged wheels ran.

Getting up steam

In England in 1825, the Stockton to Darlington line, the world's first public railroad, opened. Horses pulled most of the traffic, but from time to time, a steam locomotive was used. The engineer who provided the locomotive was George Stephenson and he named his engine Locomotion. *The engine could pull wagons crowded with hundreds of people, as well as loads of coal, iron, and corn, at 5 mph (8 kph). Soon, Stephenson and his fellow engineers designed more powerful engines.*

Business interests

In the 18th century, northeastern England was an important coal-mining area. Mine owners were anxious to sell more coal to expanding cities and industries, but moving the heavy coal was a real problem. Many of the early pioneers of steam power worked for collieries, and many mine owners gave them the money to develop their ideas. For example, Edward Pease, a Quaker businessman, helped George Stephenson and his son Robert set up a locomotive-building factory.

George Stephenson

George Stephenson, born in 1781, grew up in a cottage beside the railroad. His father was a colliery fireman. George was soon working for Nicholas Wood at Killingworth Colliery, where he began to build locomotives.

The *Rocket*

George Stephenson and his son Robert increased the engine power of the *Rocket* by leading the exhaust steam out through a narrow chimney. They also improved the heating power by passing several tubes through the iron boiler to carry the heat, instead of only one or two.

The first accident?
On September 15, 1830, the opening of the Liverpool to Manchester line was marked by tragedy. Having climbed out of one train, William Huskisson, Liverpool's Member of Parliament, was hit and killed by the *Rocket* traveling up another track.

Puffing Billy
Puffing Billy took its name from the loud noise made by its exhaust steam. Built by William Hedley it served Wylam Colliery for around 50 years. Hedley proved that smooth driving wheels running on smooth track could pull heavy loads.

The first locomotive time trials
In October 1829, an excited crowd gathered to watch four engines compete. The fastest, the *Novelty*, was built by John Braithwaite and John Ericcson, but it kept stopping. Timothy Burstall's *Perseverance* lacked power and Timothy Hackworth's *Sans Pareil* used great quantities of fuel and broke down. The Stephensons' *Rocket* steamed up and down the test track at around 14 mph (22 kph) and collected the £500 ($900.) prize.

Novelty

Sans Pareil

Making tracks
At the beginning of the 19th century, iron rails usually rested on stone supports and if any of these sank, the track became uneven. In 1820, the Englishman John Birkenshaw developed a process of making wrought iron rails that were longer than the earlier wooden rails. Stephenson adopted this improvement and, in cooperation with William Losh, designed rails that joined together by means of overlapping end sections. These joints were stronger and were pinned to the base, or the tie, which was often made of stone.

Early metal rails pinned on to ties.

A Stephenson and Losh rail

MEN AT WORK

Railroads dramatically altered the landscapes of the areas through which they passed. Inhabitants who saw railroad surveyors at work knew that close behind them followed a great army of men ready to change the look of town and country to suit the railroads. Several thousand men labored to build a main line railroad. The arrival of so many strangers often greatly alarmed the people living in the area nearby. The job of finding and organizing these workers was not easy. Railroad contractors, such as Thomas Brassey, who were good at this task were able to make a lot of money. Brassey's men built lines not only in Britain, but also in Europe, Australia, and Argentina.

Altering the landscape

Railroads need reasonably level ground to run over. Early lines had to follow the gentlest of slopes, as the locomotives of the time were not powerful enough to grip the track well on a hill. Workers cut away hilly earth, drained wet land, and built up the ground to make embankments. They cleared away housing and put up viaducts to carry railroad tracks into towns and cities.

Tools of the trade

The laborers worked with simple tools, cutting into the ground with picks, shoveling out the earth, and loading it into wheelbarrows. When faced with rock, they used gunpowder to blow it to pieces, then they hauled barrow-loads of earth and rock to horse-drawn wagons. The wagons often ran on rails to the work site, and took away earth and rock, dumping it where it was needed to make an embankment.

Barrow runs

When earth and stones were not needed, they were dumped. Horses pulled the barrows up with ropes which ran over pulleys. The men guided the barrows up the wooden planks of the barrow runs. This was a difficult task that only the strongest workers could do. A man who fell could be buried alive.

Laying track

Laying track was done in several stages. Surveyors first marked out the route (1). Next, workers leveled the land, laying a bed of small stones and putting down ties to which rails could be fixed (2). Finally, the workers fastened the rails to the ties and tested the line by running a train slowly along it (3).

The workers

In the United States, many immigrant Chinese and Irish laborers were brought in to build the railroads. The work was brutal and dangerous, and living conditions were poor. Sometimes the workers were paid no money at all, but were simply given lodgings, food, and a daily ration of whiskey.

Rapid growth

A large number of separate railroad companies built railroad lines in Britain. Early lines were quite short. The first line to cross Britain was the Carlisle to Newcastle Railway of 1838. In the late 1840s, many new lines were built. By 1850, lines linked London to Aberdeen and crossed into the West Country and Wales.

Built before 1845
Built before 1850

Aberdeen

Newcastle

Holyhead

Plymouth

London

American steam excavator built in 1843

Machine power

In the 1840s, workers were expensive to employ. To get around this problem, some contractors turned to using steam-powered machines - instead of men - to move the earth. These machines were also expensive to operate, but by 1900, excavating machines were common. In fact, two excavators and 20 men could do the same amount of work as 200 men!

A CHANGE OF GAUGE

The width of railroad track, or gauge, is not the same in every part of the world. In Britain, North America, and nearly all of Western Europe and China, the lines are 4 ft 8½ in (1,435 mm) apart. In India, Pakistan and Argentina, the width is 5ft 6 in (1,676 mm), while in Russia it is just under 5 ft (1,520 mm). There are also a number of lines that are very narrow (page 52). Early US railroads were built to a variety of gauges. By the outbreak of the Civil War in 1861, there were at least four different gauges in wide use, ranging from 4 ft 8½ in (1,435 mm) to 6 ft (1,829 mm). At the end of the war, it was decided to adopt the 4 ft 8½ in measurement as the standard gauge.

Broad gauge track of 7 ft (2,133 mm) width

The battle of the gauges
Brunel's broad gauge Great Western Railway opened in 1838. Where this line linked up to standard gauge track, passengers had to change trains. In 1845, a parliamentary commission investigated the problem, and decided in favor of the more widely used standard gauge. The GWR converted finally to standard gauge track in 1892.

Brunel argued in vain that his wider lines provided greater speed and safety.

The broad gauge
Many of the locomotives on Brunel's Great Western Railway were built by Daniel Gooch and could rush along the broad, level track at high speeds. The wide coaches could seat nine people across the width of one car, whereas standard gauge coaches only had space for five.

Enemies of the railroad

Not everyone welcomed the coming of railroads. Canal transportation suffered because train travel was much quicker. Stagecoach and wagon services were very badly hit. Three months after one local British line opened, it had put half the local stage coaches out of business! Many landowners and farmers hated the noise, smoke, and dirt and feared locomotives would frighten their animals. Some English gentry grumbled that steam engines would ruin their hunting and shooting. Even Britain's Queen Victoria - a regular train traveler - would not let a railroad travel on her land at Balmoral, Scotland.

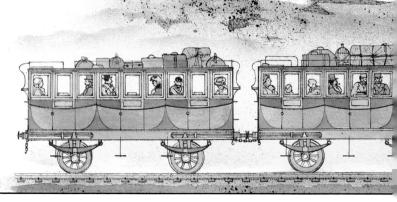

Signals

As speeds increased, warning signals became essential. Railroad managers in Britain often used officers from the army and navy to run their railroads, so they set up a network of railroad policemen who, as well as helping keep the peace, signaled to the engineers. Some used flags, others just their hands and arms.

"Caution"

"Defect on the rails"

"All clear"

Sometimes there was terrible confusion when the passengers changed trains.

The standard gauge

The 4 ft 8½ in (1,435 mm) track came about by accident. It was the gauge of many crude horse-drawn "railroads" used to transport coal in northeastern Britain, so engineers in the area, including the Stephensons, used it when building engines for local mines.

Standard gauge track

Some people were so opposed to railroad lines that they would stand in the paths of trains.

PEOPLE TRAVEL

During the second half of the 19th century, the building of railroads altered living and working conditions, and brought new opportunities for vacationing. Railroads changed the foods people ate, the clothes they wore, even the time at which they set their clocks and watches! Trains could carry large numbers of people and great quantities of goods over long distances. Those who could afford to travel by train could now live farther away from their work, and suburbs of houses with yards grew up surrounding cities. Even if they could not travel, people could still find out more about the rest of the world, for trains carried national newspapers, as well as letters and parcels.

Vacations at the shore
Wealthy people often went on vacation for many weeks, while working people enjoyed day trips or short breaks. The seashore was one of the most popular areas for vacations. Quiet little fishing villages grew in size and many hotels and guest houses were built. A number of towns added other attractions: piers, parks, and theaters.

A Victorian scene
An English railroad station around 1900 was a bustling place. Porters wheeled carts or carried passengers' suitcases and hatboxes. It was noisy and dirty, because steam trains hissed out clouds of smoke that stained the glass roofs and scattered black soot everywhere.

Timetable

In charge
The station was run by the station master. He checked the station clock for the correct "railroad time." Before railroads, different places in the same country had their own local time. These gradually vanished as railroad "standard" time took over.

14

Growth and expansion

Railroad stations rapidly developed into important centers of local life. Railroad companies began to construct large buildings, improving their appearance with beautifully decorated ironwork. Book and newspaper sellers set up stalls in the stations while new businesses opened up nearby.

Cook's tours

In 1840, Thomas Cook began organizing vacations by train all over Europe. Other people soon copied the idea. Organized sports were also popular, and people traveled to places where they could play, and to events such as soccer matches.

A better diet

Before railroads, it had not been possible to move large amounts of food because travel was so slow and costly, and fresh food rotted. Trains meant that fruit, fish, vegetables, meat, milk, and eggs could be transported easily and people's diets improved.

Porters carried passengers' luggage and helped them find the correct train to board.

HEADING WEST

Eight million people lived in the United States in the early 19th century. In the following years, many more arrived from Europe. In the 1840s, for example, over four million people poured into the country. The first railroads were built in the eastern United States, where most people had settled. But as the country's population increased, more and more people moved west, searching for more and more good land to live on and farm. The railroads spread slowly westward, too. As the demand for transportation grew, the US government was quick to support the businessmen who wanted to build railroad lines, because railroads helped to unite a vast land.

Despite the odds
Railroad builders faced all sorts of obstacles. Great mountain ranges stood in the way, deserts had to be crossed, and forests cleared. In 1856, the Rock Island Line Company tackled the vast Mississippi River. They built a huge 1,583 ft (483 m) bridge across it, opening the way west.

Setting up home
When the men who built the lines across North America moved into new areas, there were no towns or cities for them to visit, so they had to carry all they needed with them. Along the finished line, little towns grew up, with stagecoaches to carry passengers to places off the railroad line. Shops opened up and so did saloons, providing drink and entertainment.

Traveling towns
The trains themselves transported all the materials needed to build a new line. They also carried food, clothing and tools. The Union Pacific's construction crews sometimes slept in specially built "bunkhouse cars." The Union Pacific trains were often pulled by sturdy little *Pony* locomotives. These engines burned wood, as there was usually a good supply of timber nearby, and coal was harder to obtain.

Bunkhouse car

Central Pacific

Union Pacific

Across a continent

So much railroad building took place in the eastern states of North America in the 1830s that it added up to half the total track in the world. The 1839 linking of the Central Pacific and Union Pacific lines at Promontory Point, Utah, completed the coast-to-coast track.

Wagons west

Before railroads, settlers headed west had to use wagons. These were pulled by oxen or mules and traveled only 15-18 miles (25-30 km) a day. At night, the wagons were grouped in a circle for protection, with the animals in the middle. The settlers loaded the wagons with all they needed for a new life, including furniture, seeds, and stoves.

Wagons

Communications improved with the invention of the telegraph system.

Building a network

Once the main line across the continent was finished, other lines were built. In 1880, the Kansas Pacific Line was linked to the main cross-country route. Railroads meant that the inland states were opened up. Chicago, for example, was a place where eleven railroads met. Hotel-keepers there provided rooftop telescopes so their guests could look out for the arrival of important trains.

Promontory Point

The final spike, made of gold, was banged in with a silver hammer.

On May 10, 1869, a special event was organized to celebrate the linking of the Central Pacific and Union Pacific lines at Promontory Point, Utah. The Central Pacific brought a train pulled by the *Jupiter*, while the Union Pacific used *Locomotive 119*. The Union Pacific had begun work in Omaha, Nebraska, in December, 1863, using a team of workers that included 15 Native American women. Work on the Central Pacific Railroad Company had begun in January, 1863, in Sacramento, California. Laborers were in short supply there, so the line's engineers brought in thousands of Chinese laborers to do the work.

17

UNDER ATTACK

The railroads brought many benefits, but they also brought violence. The lines that spread west in the United States pushed into Native American country and the peoples who lived there soon came to hate the "iron horse" - the name they gave to the train. It frightened the wild animals and led to the killing of the great herds of buffalo the Native Americans needed for food and clothing. The advance of the Northern Pacific railroad was one of the reasons that, in 1876, Sitting Bull's Sioux attacked and defeated an army led by General Custer that was protecting work on the line. This Battle of Little Big-horn was a rare Native American success. Nothing could stop the relentless drive of the railroads.

Robbery on the plains

Wealthy people traveled by train, and many of the railroads carried gold or other valuables. Railroads soon attracted robbers and gamblers. Some waited in railroad towns to take money from travelers. Others boarded trains and robbed the passengers. Trains were even attacked while they were on the move.

Fighting back

The Native Americans tried to protect their lands and the buffalo (see above) by pulling up railroad track. Sometimes they ambushed railroad men. Workers employed by the Kansas Pacific Line learned to carry and use guns, and the company even armed their passengers as well. In 1867, Cheyenne braves ambushed a telegraph repair crew, at Plum Creek, Nebraska, and killed all but one of them. William Thompson escaped by pretending to be dead, even when he was being scalped!

Easy target

In 1870, six men boarded one of the Central Pacific trains in California. When the engine stopped for fuel and water, the men held up the train, uncoupling the engine and the express car in which valuables were stowed. They steamed farther down the track before stopping and robbing the express car.

Cut off

The telegraph wires that ran beside the track linked up stations along the way. Some trains carried telegraphers with "box relays." These men could attach the box to the wires and send messages. Outlaws attacking trains often cut the wires to stop help from being summoned.

Railroads in war

Army generals soon realized that they could use the railroad to transport men and equipment. During the American Civil War (1861-65) the northern states had a big advantage - 22,000 miles (35,200 km) of railroad against the southern states' 9,000 miles (14,400 km). Sometimes mortars such as this one were fired from the trains' flatcars.

Wanted!

Outlaws and robbers became so successful in their raids on trains that many of the railroad companies had to employ Wells Fargo agents as guards.

The famous Pinkerton's National Detective Agency was also employed to track down serial offenders such as "Butch" Cassidy and the "Sundance Kid."

A safe haven

In some areas, the railroads were unpopular because of their high prices or because they harmed local farmers or businesspeople. Outlaws in such areas could live there without fear of being turned in to the authorities.

Terrors of the track

The most feared of all robbers was a gang of outlaws led by brothers Jesse and Frank James, and their partners, the Younger boys. Their first robbery took place in 1873 in Iowa. They loosened one of the rails and tied rope around it. As the train approached they pulled the line clear, toppling the train off the tracks and killing the engineer before robbing the passengers.

19

COAST TO COAST

Inventors tried many different ways to make steam engines faster and more powerful, but the reasons the engines worked remained the same: heated water turns to steam and steam is a powerful force that can move heavy objects. This engine is the famous *Jupiter* that the Central Pacific Railroad used at Promontory Point. It had four driving wheels and four "bogey" wheels to guide the engine and keep it firmly on the track. Like many American engines,

the *Jupiter* was fitted with a cowcatcher. This was an attachment that pushed cattle off the track if they wandered into the path of a train. Cowcatchers were essential when trains crossed the Great Plains of North America.

The *Jupiter* burned wood. This did not produce as much fierce heat as coal fire, but in North America it was plentiful and cheaper than coal. Wood-burning engines often gave out a shower of sparks with the smoke and steam. The sparks could set fire to forests and dry grasslands, so "spark arresters" were fitted to the smokestacks to prevent this from happening.

Spark arrester

Lamp

Blast pipe

Cowcatcher

Steam pipe

A safety valve is built into the boiler to automatically release excess steam.

The pistons
The steam is fed down the steam pipe to two cylinders at the front of the engine. The steam is released in bursts, first at one end of the cylinders, then at the other. The force of the steam pushes the pistons backward and forward. The pistons are joined to piston rods and then to connecting rods. These link with the driving wheels, making them turn.

The boiler
The boiler is a strong metal tank filled with water. Fire tubes running through the boiler heat the water to make steam. It takes quite a while to get a steam locomotive going, as the flames in the firebox need time to build up heat in the fire tubes. More water is added from time to time as the water in the boiler is used up as it is converted to steam.

The dome
Steam from the boiler collects in the dome. The engineer driving the train decides when the steam pressure is strong enough to move the pistons and turn the wheels. He opens a valve that lets steam flow out of the dome along the steam pipe to the cylinders. Steam that has done its job of moving the pistons is released through the blast pipe.

Trekking west

Regular services across the United States began soon after the Central Pacific and Union Pacific lines were joined. The US government gave the railroad companies grants of land. These companies advertised in Europe, trying to persuade people to come to the US. They wanted to profit from carrying these people west and selling them the land. Trains such as the Jupiter *carried thousands of European immigrants to the Midwest and West Coast.*

The tender

A steam locomotive needs fuel. This is kept in a "tender," a wagon next to the engine. The fireman keeps the flames in the firebox burning by shoveling or lifting fuel onto the fire. Wood-burning locomotives such as the *Jupiter* needed large tenders in which to carry their bulky fuel and had to stop regularly to take on more.

A dangerous living

Railroad cattle towns were wild places. The railroad companies employed men to protect their cargoes in the station as well as on the journey. Abilene, Kansas, for example, was a very dangerous place to live in until James Butler Hickok became Marshall. He had already killed 43 outlaws when he earned the nickname of "Wild Bill." By the time his work in Abilene was over, he had shot 57 more criminals.

The cattle towns

Railroads helped the growth of cattle ranching. Cattle were driven up from Texas and transported quickly by train to the stockyards of Chicago and other Midwest cities. From there, the railroads took beef to the cities of the East Coast.

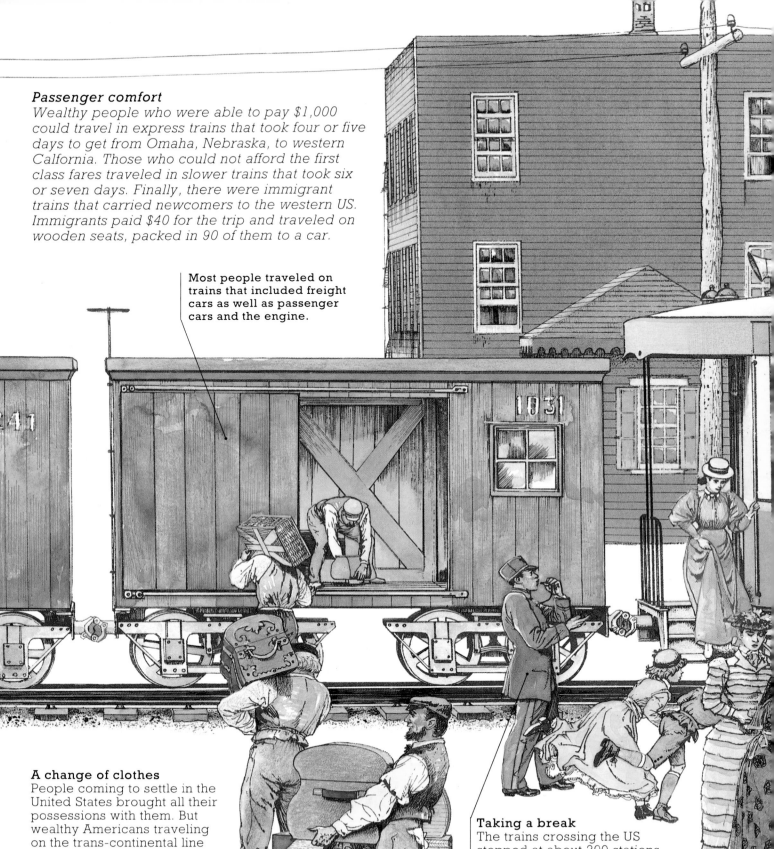

Passenger comfort
Wealthy people who were able to pay $1,000 could travel in express trains that took four or five days to get from Omaha, Nebraska, to western California. Those who could not afford the first class fares traveled in slower trains that took six or seven days. Finally, there were immigrant trains that carried newcomers to the western US. Immigrants paid $40 for the trip and traveled on wooden seats, packed in 90 of them to a car.

Most people traveled on trains that included freight cars as well as passenger cars and the engine.

A change of clothes
People coming to settle in the United States brought all their possessions with them. But wealthy Americans traveling on the trans-continental line carried plenty of luggage, too. Guide books suggested that ladies carry spring clothes for the first part of the journey west, winter clothes for use as the trains steamed over the mountains, and summer clothes for California.

Taking a break
The trains crossing the US stopped at about 200 stations and water tanks. At some of these, the passengers were allowed only 30 minutes to order and eat food. They had to listen for the conductor's whistle and cry of "All aboard!"

Basic comforts
Passengers with enough money were soon able to travel in comfortable cars designed by George Pullman. However, the cars in which settlers traveled were very basic and often had a stove at one end. Native Americans had to ride in the baggage cars, or on the steps at the ends of the cars.

Entertainment
The first railroad travelers across the continent watched wild animals and sometimes fired their guns at them. Travelers played games to pass the time. Some Pullmans had organs in them and musicians gave concerts for the passengers. On Sunday, there was usually a religious service held in one of the cars.

The travelers
In newly-settled western towns, some passengers did not bother to buy tickets first. Travelers would board a train and then argue with the conductor about how much they should pay.

23

THE CIRCUS IS COMING

The railroads brought a wide range of entertainment to the people. In England in 1796, Philip Astley put on a special show with horses and the circus was born! Others copied Astley and soon circuses and wild animal menageries went on tour. This meant walking long distances, and in much of Europe, walking caravans remained the way of travel until steam traction engines and, later, motor trucks were used. But the distances covered in North America were so huge that entertainers soon began to travel by rail instead.

In the middle of the 19th century, the great showmen Phineas Taylor Barnum and George F. Bailey developed great traveling shows that toured North America by rail and visited Europe. The "big top" show toured the US in 100-car trains.

A grand parade

Railroads meant that traveling shows could cover huge distances. New towns in the Midwest and the West Coast were especially starved of entertainment and warmly welcomed such an event. The arrival of a circus was marked by holding a big parade. This advertised the circus and was good for business.

Animal magic

People enjoyed going to see wild animals. The first tiger was brought to the United States in 1789 and the first elephant arrived in 1796. Astley's circus used trained horses and dancing bears; performing dogs and camels were also popular.

Promotion

Before a circus train arrived, posters were put up in town promising a huge variety of amazing acts - in the case of Barnum and Bailey, "A veritable Tornado of Wonders."

SALOON

Up Main Street
Some parades were more spectacular than others. In the 1860s, George Sanger's circus was touring Europe with parades of 100 horses, 42 wagons of wild animals, and a huge chariot pulled by 30 horses carrying his wife, dressed as Britannia.

ROWE AND CO's CIRCUS

DRUG STORE

Circus acts
There were all kinds of entertainers in the circuses. They included tight-rope walkers, flying trapeze artists, and clowns. The American hunter Buffalo Bill Cody recruited hundreds of Native Americans to perform in his Wild West show.

Catching the eye
Circus people tried to make their shows as spectacular as possible. The cars in which the animals traveled were highly decorated and painted. Some of them had to be very strong to transport the large and powerful animals.

An easy load
American G.R. Spalding invented special runways to load circus wagons on to railroad flatcars. W.C. Coup, who worked with Barnum and Bailey, perfected this loading and unloading technique.

THE THRILLER SUPREME

HEAVY WORK

Many industries grew up in the 19th century, as more coal and iron were mined. Heavy goods had been very difficult to move by land, so large industries needed to be by the sea, by canal, or by rivers so that boats could be used to transport goods. But railroads could reach inland to wherever they were needed, to coalfields and places where iron ore was mined. The new railroads played a major role in the Industrial Revolution, carrying heavy goods, speeding up transportation, and creating a demand for steel and iron to make new railroads. New towns grew up, like Birmingham, Alabama. By the late 19th century, Germany too, with its huge reserves of coal, was becoming a leading industrial nation, with railroads linking its industries, farmland, towns, and cities.

Industrial growth

Germany's railroads linked her iron and steel industries to her coalfields. The railroads' own need of coal and iron helped develop those industries. Some improvements to railroads benefited other industries: Krupps of Essen used the stronger steel developed for rails and wheels to make cannons.

Materials in demand

Developing industries needed huge quantities of supplies. Train loads of building materials, raw wool, jute, and cotton for textile factories, and iron ore, too, rolled endlessly into growing towns. So did the food and other supplies needed by the industrial workers.

Nasmyth's steam hammer

Iron is made stronger by being repeatedly hammered. In 1839, James Nasmyth invented a steam hammer to help Isambard Brunel (page 27) make a huge iron shaft for the paddle wheels of his ship, *Great Britain*. The steam hammer was soon being used to make iron bars for tracks in far larger quantities than the "tilt" hammers ever managed.

Products out

Many of the things made in early factories were for the railroads themselves. Locomotives, wagons, and cars were needed, so factories such as Borsig of Berlin developed. Thousands of miles of track were needed, as well as the metal parts that were bolted together to form bridges.

A changing landscape

The new industries that developed near the railroads altered the appearance of the landscape. Tall factory chimneys and the chimneys of thousands of workers' homes poured out smoke from fires supplied by trainloads of coal. Older cities changed shape as housing was razed to make room for the railroad lines. In many places, the new rail lines left thousands of people homeless.

Railroads and steamships

The British steamship the *Great Eastern* first set sail in 1858. The great railroad bridge builder Isambard Kingdom Brunel designed this vessel, but died eight days after the launch. The idea of using steam to move ships developed at much the same time as the steam locomotive. Paddle wheels were used at first, and continued to be useful on rivers and lakes. But in rough seas, they tipped out of the water, so propellers proved more reliable. Railroads helped make steamships successful by bringing people and goods to the ports.

Workers

Railroads employed huge numbers of people, including thousands who lived in railroad towns where engines were made and repaired. Workers' lives began to be ruled by machines. Yet by bringing a wide variety of cheaper food and cheap clothing, railroads improved people's standard of living.

27

STRANGE TRAINS

Extraordinary engines had to be designed to solve unusual problems. Where railroad lines climbed up and down steep slopes and crossed deep gorges, engineers often had to think up unusual designs for their engines (pages 52-53). The search for speed led to the building of locomotives with enormous driving wheels, because a piston can turn a big wheel as quickly as a small wheel, but a big wheel travels farther. On the American Baltimore and Ohio Railroad, engines were run that looked much like camels! They had a "hump" - the driver's cab - placed right on top of a long and narrow boiler.

The engineers who struggled to design the first locomotives sometimes came up with very odd inventions. The Englishman William Brunton amazed people in 1815 with a steam locomotive pushed along the rails by two huge legs, complete with ankle joints and feet. Unfortunately, on one disastrous day it blew up, killing its crew and several people who were looking closely at it.

An odd assortment
These two pages show some of the more unusual engines and railroad tracks of the 19th century. Although peculiar they were all invented to solve particular sets of problems. All ran successfully for a number of years and some were even copied.

Trains with teeth
When track has to be built up and down very steep slopes, ordinary wheels slip and slide too easily. Early engineers designed an extra rail in a rack shape - a cog wheel with teeth fitted into projections on the rack. Rack railroad systems were especially popular in Switzerland.

This steam-powered "rack and pinion" train is one of two that operate today in Austria.

The "Daddy Long Legs"
Imagine a train that has to be fitted with lifeboats and life belts! In 1896, just such a train ran at Brighton, in England. The track along which it ran was 18 ft (5,486 mm) wide and nearly 3 miles (4.4 km) long, and it carried its passengers through 15 ft (4.5 m) of sea water. It was built by Magnus Volk and ran for five years before the damage caused by rough water battering the rails led to the line being abandoned.

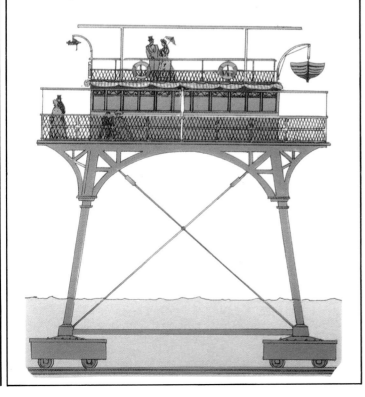

Ireland's Listowel to
Ballybunion line ran
from 1888 to 1924.

Running on one rail

When the French
inventor Charles Lartigue
proposed a cheap form of track
in 1883, there was great interest.
Lartigue supported a single rail on an
A-shaped frame. Engines rode along the
track, with supports on either side to prevent
them from tipping over. Lines such as this were built
in France, North Africa, Russia, Peru, and
Guatemala as well as this example from Ireland.

A double engine

In 1836, the Ffestiniog Railway
opened, linking slate quarries on
the coast of Wales. Horses were
used until 1863, when steam
locomotives took over. The heavy
loads were pulled by powerful
engines with two boilers called
Double Fairlies. In 1865, this
railroad became the world's
first passenger-carrying
narrow gauge line.

Elevated lines

In the late 19th
century, some
New Yorkers living
at third floor level
were able to watch
engines steaming past
their windows. The city was
the setting for the world's first
elevated railroad. The line was
enormously popular, some sections
carrying 1,000 trains a day, pulled
by 0-4-4 Forney tank engines.

THE AGE OF ROMANCE

On October 4, 1883, a Belgian businessman walked anxiously up and down the platform of a Paris railroad station. His name was Georges Nagelmackers and he had just risked all his money paying for the building of a brand new train. He planned to run this train right across Europe by using the tracks of several countries. Many people told him this would be impossible because it would mean persuading bickering countries to agree to the plan. Moreover, the fare on Nagelmackers' train was extremely expensive.

The Compagnie Internationale des Wagons Lits, Nagelmackers' company, was set up in 1876. By 1883, Nagelmackers had permission to take his train across eastern Europe to the Black Sea coast. The new train was called the *Orient Express*, a title that attracted great interest among wealthy travelers seeking adventure. So many secret agents used the train that it earned the nickname of the "Spies Express." The spies included the dancer Mata Hari, a German spy; and two agents who were killed by being pushed out of the moving cars.

An elegant meal
Nagelmackers attached an elegant restaurant car to his first train and soon established a tradition of serving fine food and wines. The passengers dined wearing expensive clothes in a car lit by huge chandeliers; this tradition continues today. These pages show passengers on board the train in the 1920s.

At risk
Traveling on the *Orient Express* was not without danger. In 1901, the train crashed into the crowded restaurant hall at Frankfurt station. Amazingly, no one was hurt. Some years later, huge snowdrifts trapped the train for several days until Turkish soldiers dug it out. The most alarming incident of all was the 1891 deliberate derailing of the train. As passengers struggled to their feet, a gang of bandits led by a huge bearded man burst in and robbed them.

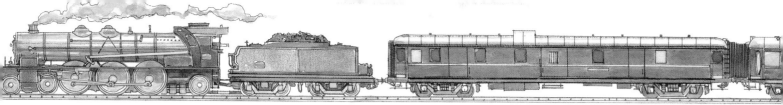

Engine   **Tender**   **Baggage car**

Food and drink
The first restaurant meal on the *Orient Express* was prepared on a gas stove in a tiny kitchen by a chef, three under-chefs, three handymen, and two dishwashers. Today, the kitchen has the benefit of new technology, but it is still just as small.

Dressing up
The waiters serving meals on the first trip made by the *Orient Express* wore powdered wigs, tailcoats, breeches, and silk stockings. However, passengers soon complained that the powder from the wigs fell into their food!

Decor
No expense was spared in fitting out the *Orient Express*. Paneling of the finest woods was carved into fanciful shapes. In the compartments, the armchairs were covered in soft Spanish leather while some of the walls were covered in silk.

The train
Nagelmackers provided the coaches, but the locomotives pulling them were owned by the different railroad companies along whose track the train ran. The engines needed to be powerful, as the train had to move at high speed.

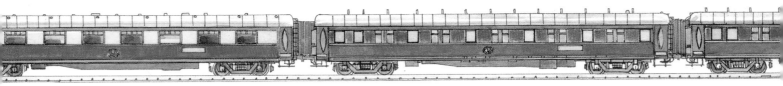

Restaurant car

Sleeping compartments

The Orient Express *in the 20th century*
During the World War I (1914-18), the Orient Express *could not run, and World War II (1939-45) again stopped its services. When the train ran again, many people were traveling by air instead. In 1977, the* Orient Express *stopped operations altogether, but in 1982 it was realized that there was still a market for such a famous train. Old cars were rescued from sidings in France and Britain, and lovingly restored.*

Advertising
The train's name and the places it visited made possible very attractive advertising. This poster advertises a route from Calais to the south of France that began in 1883. *Le Train Bleu* provided its travelers with the world's first traveling cocktail bar.

Comforts of home
The early cars had a toilet cabinet with marble fixtures. Later, a fully-equipped bathroom was added, containing towels embroidered with the *Orient Express* logo.

Ticket collectors wore a distinctive blue uniform.

At night
Nagelmackers divided his coaches into sleeping compartments, in which there were two beds covered in silk sheets, wool blankets, and down comforters. Each compartment had a bell for calling the attendant.

Railway routes

At first the *Orient Express* traveled from Paris by way of southern Germany, Vienna, and Budapest. At the Danube River, a ferry was used and the journey ended on the shores of the Black Sea. By 1899, it was possible to stay on board all the way to Constantinople, now Istanbul. Later, travelers wanting to go beyond Istanbul took the *Taurus Express*, bound for Tripoli.

This map shows the route used after World War I. The *Orient Express* traveled into Italy through the Alps, via the Simplon Tunnel.

London
Brussels
Berlin
Prague
Paris
Lausanne
Bordeaux
Venice
Budapest
Belgrade
Sofia
BLACK SEA
Ankara
MEDITERRANEAN SEA
Bagdad
Bassora
Cairo

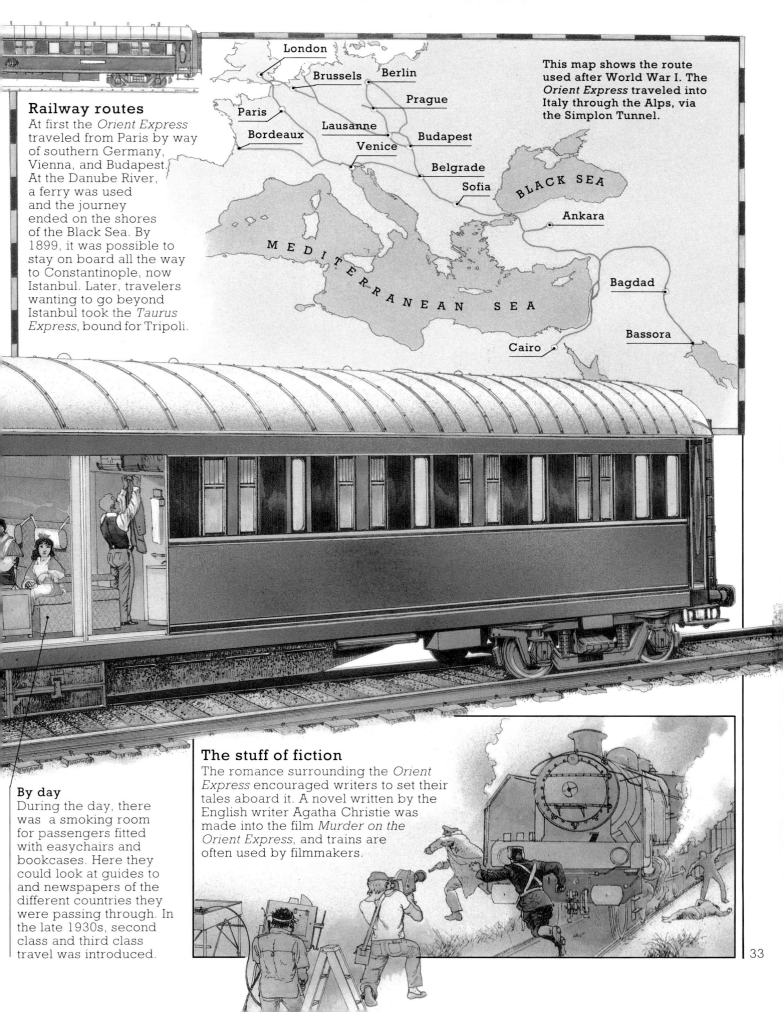

By day

During the day, there was a smoking room for passengers fitted with easychairs and bookcases. Here they could look at guides to and newspapers of the different countries they were passing through. In the late 1930s, second class and third class travel was introduced.

The stuff of fiction

The romance surrounding the *Orient Express* encouraged writers to set their tales aboard it. A novel written by the English writer Agatha Christie was made into the film *Murder on the Orient Express*, and trains are often used by filmmakers.

A POWER RACE

Steam locomotives were costly to maintain and required huge quantities of coal. They usually had to stop to pick up water, and the smoke that poured from their stacks spattered people with soot and stained buildings. For many years, inventors searched for other sources of power to pull trains. They found the answers to the problems of steam in diesel engines and electric motors.

End of an era

Diesel and electric locomotives first appeared in the 19th century, and by the 1930s were becoming very popular. By the 1940s and 1950s, steam power was being replaced on a massive scale. The J 4-8-4 below was built for the Norfolk and Western Railroad in the United States. The last steam locomotive for that line was built in 1953.

10201

The pantograph picks up electricity from overhead wires.

Diesel-electric locomotives
This diesel-electric is a British mainline locomotive of the late 1940s. Dr. Rudolf Diesel, who died in 1913, pioneered the diesel engine. In 1930, the giant American car manufacturer, General Motors, began to make large numbers of reliable diesel units. The diesel engine powers an electric generator. This generator then supplies electric traction motors that in turn power the axles. The engines are costly to build, but more efficient to run than steam engines.

Electric power
Countries that lacked rich coalfields, such as Switzerland and Sweden, welcomed the chance to use electricity. The power is usually carried in overhead wires, and picked up by engines like this one used on Swedish Railways in the 1940s. Sometimes power is carried on a third rail. It is expensive to supply the lines that carry the current. But electricity provides a cleaner, more reliable, and more powerful form of transportation.

The leading wheels guide and support the engine.

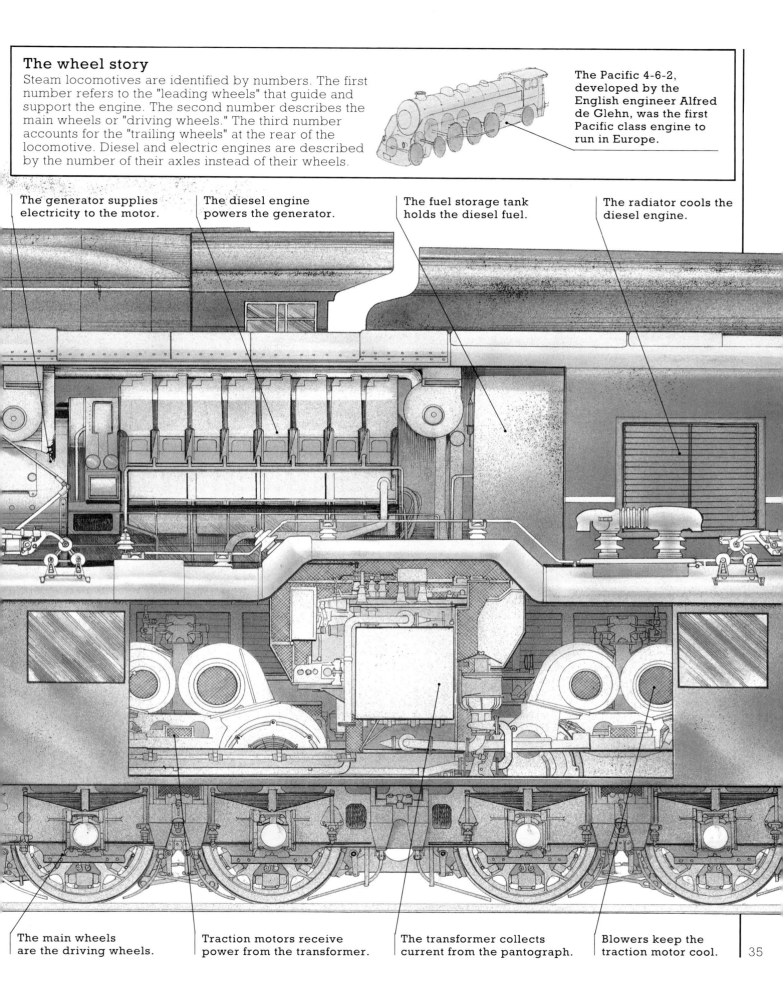

The wheel story

Steam locomotives are identified by numbers. The first number refers to the "leading wheels" that guide and support the engine. The second number describes the main wheels or "driving wheels." The third number accounts for the "trailing wheels" at the rear of the locomotive. Diesel and electric engines are described by the number of their axles instead of their wheels.

The Pacific 4-6-2, developed by the English engineer Alfred de Glehn, was the first Pacific class engine to run in Europe.

The generator supplies electricity to the motor.

The diesel engine powers the generator.

The fuel storage tank holds the diesel fuel.

The radiator cools the diesel engine.

The main wheels are the driving wheels.

Traction motors receive power from the transformer.

The transformer collects current from the pantograph.

Blowers keep the traction motor cool.

LAST GASP

Steam locomotives could only hold their own against diesel and electric trains if engineers could find a way to make their trains go faster. The Swiss inventor Anatole Mallet worked at increasing the power produced by the steam engine. In 1876, Mallet invented the "compound engine." Instead of going straight to the blastpipe and stack, steam leaving the cylinder passed first to a low pressure cylinder, thus providing additional power. In 1891, the German engineer, Wilhelm Schmidt, devised the "superheater." An arrangement of pipes led the steam through a chamber containing hot gases from the firebox, so increasing the temperature. When Mallet's and Schmidt's ideas were brought together, they led to the building of the most efficient steam expresses ever seen.

Racing along

In 1893, Locomotive 999 had managed a speed of 112 mph (180 kph), on New York Central's line. By May 1936, a German steam locomotive hauling a train on the Berlin-Hamburg line reached 124 mph (199.2 kph). Railroad companies in every country competed with one another to provide the fastest trains, trying to attract travelers to steam travel by offering the excitement of speed.

The *Flying Scotsman*
One of the most famous locomotives in the world, the *Flying Scotsman,* was designed by Sir Nigel Gresley for the LNER, and is still brought out to impress audiences today. From 1928, it provided a world record non-stop service over the 392 miles (632 km) between London and Edinburgh. The *Flying Scotsman* scooped up water from troughs in the track as it rushed along so that it would not have to stop.

The *Mallard*
The lines of the London and North Eastern Railway (LNER) lay up the eastern side of Britain; its chief engineer was Sir Nigel Gresley. In the 1930s, he decided that if he fitted streamlined casing over his locomotives, it would increase their speed. In 1938, the *Mallard,* one of these new high-speed engines, reached a speed of 126 mph (203 kph) while pulling a seven-coach train down a gradient. This has remained the world record for steam-hauled trains.

The *Hiawatha*
This famous American train was specially built to provide high-speed passenger travel across the United States. The service began in 1935 on the Chicago, Milwaukee, St. Paul, and Pacific Line. The 409 miles (660 km) from Chicago to St. Paul was covered in just 5 hours 5 minutes. The train's average speed was 82 mph (131.5 kph), though it reached a top speed of 105 mph (168 kph).

Big Boy
Big Boys were the largest and most powerful steam locomotives in the world. Built for the Union Pacific Railroad in the United States, they first appeared in 1941. Each locomotive weighed 350 tons and carried with it 21,000 gallons (95,466 liters) of water. *Big Boys* were based on the ideas of Anatole Mallet.

Garrett engines
The Englishman Herbert William Garrett was an engineer who tried to make bigger locomotives. A giant-sized engine was too heavy for the track and had difficulty cornering. In 1907, Garrett produced a single boiler placed between two engine units, with water on one and fuel on the other. This spread the weight and allowed the engine to travel around sharp curves.

UP FRONT

In 1908, Henry Ford produced a cheap, reliable car - the Model T - that he made in great numbers. This marked the start of a new transportation revolution. Cars, trucks and buses began to pour off the assembly lines of factories in Europe and North America. They provided door-to-door travel that was more convenient than going by train. By 1917, there were nearly five million cars in the United States and the US government began an extensive road-building program to support the extra vehicles. In Europe, too, new roads were built, including an early highway system in Germany. At the same time, railroad companies faced another threat: air travel had developed into a reliable and fast service.

At first, the railroad companies replied by

The engineer sits in a cab right on top of the *Settebello.*

The American *Zephyr*
On May 26, 1934, the Burlington Railroad Company's new diesel-powered train *Pioneer Zephyr* made a record-breaking run. The *Zephyr* hurtled over the 1,017-mile (1,637 km) route between Chicago and Denver in just over 13 hours - half the time of previous records! This success marked the arrival of long-distance "streamliner" services in the US. In the same year, the rival Union Pacific introduced its own version, the M.1000.

The Italian *Settebello*
Imagine traveling on a train that looked like an airplane! This was the exciting possibility that Italian State Railways offered to travelers in 1953. Its *Settebello* service hurtled up and down the line that linked Milan to Rome. The engineer sat in a kind of cockpit above the passenger coach so that passengers could enjoy clear views forward and backward along the route. This popular and luxurious service was part of the TEE service.

providing more luxurious travel. In the 1930s, the increased use of diesel and electric locomotives helped them to run cleaner and more reliable services. After World War II (1939-45), railroad companies found it harder to compete and turned to their governments for support. In the United States, Amtrak was set up with government help to run intercity passenger services across the country.

High-speed efficiency

Powerful, streamlined, diesel-powered locomotives began to appear in North America and Europe. In 1957, a network linking Europe's main cities, the Trans-European Express, was set up. The TEE service covered nine countries, with 35 trains operating 27 different routes. High-speed luxury passenger services became popular worldwide.

The TEE coaches are made from stainless steel.

Amtrak Metroliners averaged more than 90 mph (144 kph).

The *Rheingold*
In 1928, the German *Rheingold* was one of Europe's great express services. Since 1965, this train has become part of the TEE network. Originally it was hauled by steam locomotives, then by diesels, but now it is powered by electricity. Its journey begins in Amsterdam and continues through Holland across Germany and into Austria. Its passengers travel in great comfort in soundproofed coaches made of stainless steel.

Amtrak
In the United States there are enormous distances to cover, long trains to be pulled, and steep climbs through the Rocky Mountains. This all means that powerful locomotives are needed. In 1971, the organization Amtrak was set up with money from the government to provide a high-speed passenger service from city to city. Amtrak ran the new United Aircraft Turbotrains, which were diesel, as well as the electric Metroliners.

39

THE TRAIN NOW BOARDING...

The India Railway Board controls lines that make up the biggest railroad network in Asia and the fourth biggest in the world. There are 37,700 miles (60,320 km) of track which include main lines built to a broad gauge of 5 ft 6 in (1,981mm), local lines built to a 3 ft 3 in gauge (1 meter), and narrow gauge lines as well. Indian railroads are very popular, with over ten million people traveling on them each day. To serve these passengers, the railroad has more than 7,000 stations. Some are simple wooden platforms and huts, while vast and splendid buildings serve the cities. One of the biggest, Howrah Station, was built in 1906 in Calcutta. The Victoria Terminus at Bombay is one of the grandest stations in the world. It is decorated with domes, stained glass windows, and sculptures.

A meeting place

Indian railroad stations are very important centers of local and national life. Huge numbers of people gather in them to wait for trains, to meet friends and family, or to buy and sell all sorts of things. The larger stations include restaurants and waiting rooms, where passengers with tickets may sit or stretch out and sleep.

Ticket offices

Because the Indian railroads are so popular, ticket offices often have very long lines. It is not unusual for Indian travelers to arrive many hours before their train is to depart - sometimes even days - and sleep in the station. But second-class travel in India is one of the cheapest in the world.

Class division

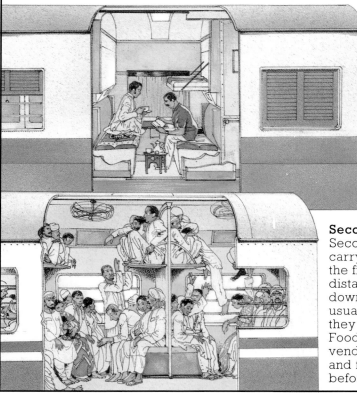

First-class travel

Indian passenger trains are divided into classes. The faster main line trains include first-class compartments with two or four berths. Many of these cars are air-conditioned and some have private showers and toilets. Only wealthy Indians and tourists can afford to travel in such comfort and eat in the restaurant cars.

Second-class travel

Second-class compartments carry far more people than the first class ones. On long distance trains, the seats fold down into bunks. Passengers usually bring bedding, though they can rent it in the station. Food can be bought from vendors who walk back and forth past the cars before the train leaves.

Shops

In stations across the world, travelers will find book and newspaper shops, restaurants, and shops selling snacks. Such places help pass the time, both for passengers about to travel, and for those waiting to meet people arriving by train.

Timetables

The huge Indian railroad network is complicated. The system is divided into seven separate zones, each with its own timetable. Travelers need to ask the station porters to help them find their trains.

A hive of activity

For some people, stations are places where most of their lives are spent. While some people sleep, others roam around trying to sell goods. Since Hindu beliefs include a special respect for cows, these animals may wander in to stations looking for food.

On the track

Electric or diesel locomotives pull mainline express and mail trains. However, steam engines are still used to pull some of the trains that run on the slower local lines. These trains are a part of local life. When there is no room for goods inside the train, they often carry them on the roofs of the goods wagons.

EN ROUTE

The first train passengers had to be tough. Third-class passengers traveled in open wagons with holes drilled in the floor so that downpours of rain could drain away. But railroad companies soon learned that taking care of passengers meant far more people would travel on their trains. In 1863, George Mortimer Pullman built a coach called the *Pioneer* that was very comfortable to travel in. However, it cost four times as much as other coaches, and railroad companies did not buy Pullman's coaches until two years later - 1865.

Candles and oil lamps lit up early coaches. In 1850, a US company introduced gas lighting and by 1885 the first electric lights were in use. Seating improved too, though early travelers on Japanese trains, who were used to sitting on rush matting, found the padded seats unusual. Heating also improved. Early passengers shivered through chilly regions, but in 1881 steam heating was introduced in US passenger cars.

Modern travel

Today, passenger comfort and the transportation of goods has improved, but trains have had to face competition from car and bus travel. In the 1960s in Europe and the United States, the numbers of passengers fell sharply. Now the rising cost of fuel and public awareness of car pollution have helped the railroads recover.

Many Indian travelers ride on the carriage roofs.

Sleepers

Most modern trains offer travelers a sleeper service. On European trains, beds are fitted in air-conditioned coaches which are also soundproofed. Many of the sleeping compartments have sinks, and some sleeping cars are equipped with toilets. Attendants take care of the passengers and bring them refreshments.

Seats fold down to make beds at night.

Travel through India

Steam trains are still common in India, and traveling by train in India is not expensive. The railroads are very popular and passengers crowd onto the trains as best they can, particularly on short journeys. Some people try to travel without paying by jumping onto the cars as the train sets off. These travelers have to hang on to the windows and handrails. The wind and rain, the heat of the burning sun, and clouds of dust often make their journeys quite dangerous.

Wheels on wheels

Over the centuries, many different kinds of railroad cars have been designed to transport all shapes and sizes of freight. Car-transporters are used by some carmakers to send their vehicles out to the showrooms. Such transportation forms a large part of the freight business here in the United States. The transporters are also widely used by people who want to take their cars with them on vacation, but do not want the long, tiring drive to their destination.

Car-transporters are loaded by driving the cars up ramps.

There were fold-away sleeping berths above the seats.

A Pullman coach of the 1880s

Pullman coaches

Pullman's coaches were very well built; they were decorated with polished wood, brass, and other fine materials. They were equipped with toilets and sinks and Pullman developed a sleeping berth that folded away in his first sleeping cars. These proved very popular for long journeys across the United States, and railroads in other countries adopted the idea. Curtains were pulled across at night to separate the sleeping travelers from each other. There were comfortable sofas for passengers to sit on by day.

A variety of uses

Modern railroad companies must think of new ways of attracting customers. For the passenger, this can mean more comfortable cars or different ways of passing the traveling time. For the freight companies, the main interest is in a faster, more efficient service.

The "vista dome," invented by the Canadian T. J. McBride, is built above the main body of the car.

A clear view

Many trains travel through beautiful scenery, and one of the pleasures of travel is the opportunity to admire the landscape through which the train is traveling. Some trains are designed with observation cars to give passengers an uninterrupted view. In 1902, the Canadian Pacific Railway introduced cars fitted with special viewing areas called "vista domes."

Sorting it out

Cheap and fast letter and parcel delivery became possible when, in 1838, the first traveling post office ran along a railroad. Soon the mail was being sorted by workers in specially-designed cars. But eventually, train robbers and the growth of large sorting offices led to the end of this method of sorting.

Loading crane

Container transportation

New ways of moving goods have been invented to combat the use of road transportation. One is the use of containers. These are usually large boxes that are filled with goods at the factory, then carried by truck to rail container-loading centers (page 57). Special cranes pick up the containers and move them onto flatcars. They can then be carried to wherever they are needed. The biggest container port in Europe is a railcenter, Bremerhaven in Germany. The success of such ports shows how railroads are still essential in the network of goods transportation.

A container is lifted from the back of a truck onto a flatcar.

Catching the mail

In the early days of the railroad, the mail was loaded onto trains only when the train was in a station. Then came an invention that did away with these stops. The mail was placed in bags and hung on hooks alongside the track. As the trains went speeding past, they used special nets to scoop up the mail bags and drop off sorted mail for local distribution.

The mail-vans of the traveling post offices (TPOs) are attached to fast passenger trains.

The way forward?

French railroads have made great efforts to attract customers. Their SNCF network can provide many different kinds of coaches that can be ordered for special events. These include a dance-car that has a dance floor, a bar, special loudspeakers and lighting, and a lounge area. Customers can also hire a movie theater that seats sixty people and a conference room coach.

CITY TRAVEL

Until the second half of the 19th century, Japan had kept itself separate from the rest of the world. Then the Japanese began to trade with other countries. This led to the development of industries, including shipbuilding and the manufacture of steel. In 1872, a railroad line opened between Tokyo and Yokohama. By 1880, most cities in Japan were linked by rail.

During the 20th century, the population of Japan has grown in size. Because almost three quarters of the country is mountainous, and much of it is covered in forest, expanding towns and cities have had to crowd into coastal areas. On the main island of Honshu, a long narrow strip that includes cities such as Tokyo and Osaka houses most of the population. A first-class public travel network is essential to the country.

A teeming population

About 123 million people live in Japan, and three quarters of them are city dwellers. One district of Tokyo, Shinjuku, contains one of the world's busiest stations. Nine different railroad and underground lines come together there, and more than two million people pass through the station every day.

Underground

There are underground railroad systems in most of Japan's major cities, such as Tokyo and Osaka. Tokyo's lines were begun in the 1920s and form an extensive system. Few parts of the city are more than five minutes from a subway station. The underground is heavily used, with about five million people crowding on it every day. During rush hours, the system employs broad-shouldered officials in uniforms and white gloves whose job it is to push as many people as possible onto the trains.

Changing track

Today, there is an extensive program of track-laying in Japan to widen the many narrow gauge lines to carry modern trains. The very mountainous landscape had caused the original engineers to recommend a narrow gauge of 3 ft 6 in (1,066 mm).

The rail network

During the 20th century, Japan Railways has developed under the control of the government. Today, it has about 13,106 miles (21,091 km) of 3 ft 6 in (1,066 mm) track, about a quarter of which has been electrified. Recently, it has been split up into seven companies, and is increasingly run by private groups.

Chinese railroads

China is an enormous country and railroads provide a crucial link between distant cities. The first permanent line was built to connect Shanghai and Woosung in 1880.

Railroads developed as many separate lines. Since 1949, the People's Republic of China has been linking these together to form a single network. Parts of the country are rich in coal, so Chinese railroads still make use of steam-powered locomotives such as the huge 2-10-2 Class QJs.

Track-laying in China

Fast as a bullet

The first high-speed *shinkansen* route connected Tokyo to Osaka in 1965. The "bullet" trains hurtle along their own standard gauge track and provide the passengers with quiet travel, but they make a deafening noise for people living near the line. Now, the railroad company reduces noise levels by making the trains run between special trackside walls shaped like inverted Ls.

Rail services

Trains are color-coded to help passengers find the correct one. There are local (*futsu*) services, rapid (*kalsoleu*) trains, expresses (*kyuko*), and an additional kind of express service (*tokkyu*) that only makes limited stops. One line loops around Tokyo, with 29 stops in all; other tracks crisscross the city.

GOING UNDERGROUND

As cities grew, their buildings spread out over more and more land. Cities became so huge that walking to work, to the stores, and to restaurants became increasingly difficult in streets crowded with horse-drawn vehicles.

Engineers realized that the answer lay in underground railroads. In 1863, the first such line opened in London. In 1900, the Paris Metro and the New York subway opened, and many other cities around the world followed suit. The development of cars, motor buses, and trucks slowed down building during the early 1900s, but today interest in underground railroads has revived. Motor traffic brings noise, pollution, traffic jams, and the destruction of buildings to create roads and parking lots. Underground trains can carry more people without causing this damage.

An expanding network
Between 1960 and 1990, about 12 new underground lines were built every five years. Today, 35 cities are building, or planning to build, new lines. These works include a huge project to construct 101 miles (163 km) in Beijing, China. Trains have to be carefully monitored because so many rush at high speeds through the tunnels.

Travel by "tube"
The cut-and-fill method of construction (see below) is only possible near the surface. In 1870, the first "tube" was opened. The track ran inside a metal tube beneath London's Thames River. Today, lines are dug at many different depths.

Ticket office

New lines in a system can be placed in tubes that pass above or below older lines.

Better safe than sorry
At first, some people were afraid that there would be accidents, while others worried about fire underground or that they would not be able to breathe properly. Companies installed ventilator shafts and fans, alarms on trains and, more recently, closed-circuit television.

The first underground
In London in 1863, the Metropolitan and District Railway opened the first underground in the world. It was made by digging a deep trench in the street, supporting the trench sides with walls and making a roof of brick arches and iron girders. The street was then replaced. This method is called cut-and-fill. The engineer in charge, John Fowler, used a steam locomotive called *Fowler's Ghost* to pull the cars.

Ventilator shaft

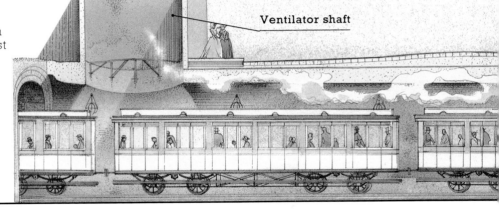

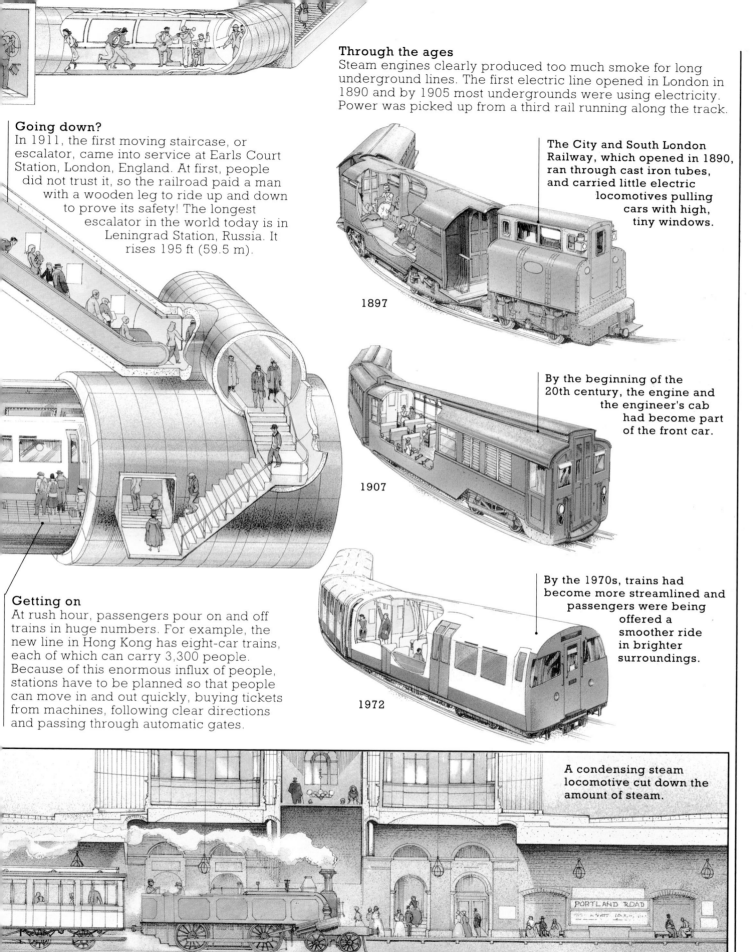

Through the ages

Steam engines clearly produced too much smoke for long underground lines. The first electric line opened in London in 1890 and by 1905 most undergrounds were using electricity. Power was picked up from a third rail running along the track.

The City and South London Railway, which opened in 1890, ran through cast iron tubes, and carried little electric locomotives pulling cars with high, tiny windows.

1897

Going down?

In 1911, the first moving staircase, or escalator, came into service at Earls Court Station, London, England. At first, people did not trust it, so the railroad paid a man with a wooden leg to ride up and down to prove its safety! The longest escalator in the world today is in Leningrad Station, Russia. It rises 195 ft (59.5 m).

By the beginning of the 20th century, the engine and the engineer's cab had become part of the front car.

1907

Getting on

At rush hour, passengers pour on and off trains in huge numbers. For example, the new line in Hong Kong has eight-car trains, each of which can carry 3,300 people. Because of this enormous influx of people, stations have to be planned so that people can move in and out quickly, buying tickets from machines, following clear directions and passing through automatic gates.

By the 1970s, trains had become more streamlined and passengers were being offered a smoother ride in brighter surroundings.

1972

A condensing steam locomotive cut down the amount of steam.

PORTLAND ROAD

TUNNELS AND TUNNELING

Long stretches of the world's railroads lie inside tunnels. Tunnels can be made in a number of ways. Those close to the surface are often built by cut-and-fill: digging a deep trench, building walls and roofing, then filling in the trench (pages 48-49). Deeper tunnels cannot be created like this. They have to be bored or hacked out from rock and clay well below the surface. Where a tunnel is to be laid on the bed of a large river or under the sea, a level trench is sometimes dredged out, and sections of tubing lowered from barges into the trench. Divers fasten the sections together, then seal the joints. A tunnel made like this carries trains 130 ft (40 m) below the surface of San Francisco Bay in California. Tunnels through mountains are usually built as shown in this scene.

Deep underground
The many stages of work shown here would, in reality, be spread across a considerable distance. The building method used is known as drill-and-blast. Hard rock is shifted by blowing it to pieces with explosives placed in drill holes. The workers are using the bench method in which the top half of the tunnel is finished first.

Safety first
Tunneling has always been dangerous. Modern workers wear hard hats to protect themselves from injury. Yet rock and earth falls can bury them, and water may burst in and sweep them away. The workers also need a supply of fresh air. This comes from ventilation shafts drilled down into the tunnel, and from pumped-in air.

Early tunneling
The men who built the first railroad tunnels hacked at rock with picks and blew it up with gunpowder. The machine shown here marked a big step forward. It was designed by an Italian, Germains Sommeiller, to cut the Fréjus tunnel 5 miles (12 km) through a mountain to link French and Italian railroad lines. He developed a drill powered by compressed air, and fitted several of these drills to a wheeled car.

Moving materials
The rock and earth that has been dug away is called spoil. It is continuously cleared away or "mucked out" as tunneling proceeds. Special machines often fitted with sound-proofed cabs do this work.

Drilling and blasting
Machines like these are called "jumbos." They are actually a modern development of Sommeiller's invention. A jumbo is fitted with several drills, each of which is mounted on a movable arm. The drills bore holes that are usually about 10 ft (3 m) deep into the hard rock. Explosive charges are then placed in the holes.

Lining the tunnel

Usually, modern tunnels have to be lined. This keeps the tunnel free from inrushes of water and prevents falls of loose material. These workers are spraying the walls with a liquid concrete mixture that will set hard. A mixer pump delivers the liquid up pipes to the operators. The process is known as "shotcreting."

Rock bolts help support the tunnel walls.

Recycled material

The mucking-out machines gather up the spoil, dumping it in earth-moving equipment that takes it away. Sometimes the spoil is stored temporarily until it can be used to build up the level of the track. Liquid waste is pumped out through pipes. With tunnel-boring machines (see below) the spoil is automatically removed by conveyor belt.

Tunnel-boring machines

The latest tunnels are made with tunnel-boring machines (TBMs). These machines have been used to build the 33-mile (54 km) Seikan tunnel under the sea between the Japanese islands of Honshu and Hokkaido. They have also cut three 31-mile (50 km) tunnels joining France to Britain. Laser beams guide the TBMs along the correct route.

The front of a TBM is fitted with huge blades that spin around, pressed forward by hydraulic rams.

OVERCOMING OBSTACLES

The land that railroads have to cross is sometimes too hilly and steep to be shaped for track simply by cutting away rock and earth. Where railroads cross rivers and estuaries, the building problems are sometimes complicated to solve. When George Stephenson (page 8) built the line from Manchester to Liverpool in England in 1830, he had to construct as many as 63 bridges, as well as a viaduct to carry track over a canal. During the last 150 years, different building techniques have been developed to cross different obstacles. For example, the methods used to build a bridge over a deep, narrow gorge are very different from those used to built a viaduct over a wide valley.

Up and over

Sometimes, railroad builders deliberately choose to build lines up very steep mountains because passengers are attracted by the view and by the excitement of the journey. These pages show some of the ingenious ways in which railroad engineers have overcome the greatest obstacles.

The "rack" railroad

In 1889, the world's steepest "rack" railroad opened. It runs up Mount Pilatus in Switzerland, on a system designed by Edward Locher. The rack is a long center rail with teeth on either side that are gripped firmly by the train, preventing it from slipping backward.

Pushing on

The engines that power the Pilatus line are very powerful and push the trains up the steep gradients. The early locomotives were steam-powered, but from 1937, electric engines have been used. The passengers travel in cars that are specially designed to fit the angle of the slope.

Bridges

Early bridge builders had to use simple methods and tools, and basic materials. But modern machinery and the use of better building materials have led to the development of a great variety of designs.

Viaduct: a many-arched span needed to cross a lengthy area of low land

Arch: a strong single span, made from stone, brick, concrete, or metal

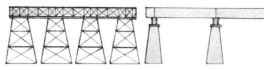

Trestle: a bridge supported by trestles, which are networks of wood or metal

Girder: steel girder sections that meet at, and rest on strong stone or brick pillars

Cantilever: balanced and linked bridge sections resting on strong supports

Narrow gauge lines

Narrow gauge lines twist and turn up and down mountains where the slopes do not need rack or cable. This is the Rhaetian Railway in Switzerland which opened in 1889. It carries people to popular winter skiing resorts. Here, it is crossing the Landwasser Viaduct, which is 213 ft (65 m) high.

Funiculars

Ordinary railroads cannot make very steep climbs, but cable or funicular railroads can. There are usually two tracks with a car on each. The cables are wound around stationary engines at each end and the weight of one car being lowered is used to pull the other one up the slope.

Avalanche!

Heavy snowfalls in mountainous areas can loosen snow and cause avalanches. Railroad lines are often protected by concrete roofing, which allows the snow to sweep harmlessly over the track. In the United States, the Santa Fe's *El Capitan* passes through shelters like these.

Building bridges

On December 28, 1879, part of a huge cast-iron bridge across the Tay River in Scotland collapsed. The crew of a train and 73 passengers died. This disaster was a terrible warning to engineers: future bridges must be built properly, and checked and repaired regularly.

Trestle bridges

There are many trestle bridges in the United States. Early railroad builders used the plentiful supplies of timber because the trestle design suited this material. During the Civil War, builders such as Herman Haupt became skillful at replacing damaged trestle bridges quickly.

Maintaining and repairing

Heavy trains hurtling along at rapid speed shake track loose. Storms, floods, and landslides can also damage the line. Early track repair kept great numbers of workers busy. Modern machines such as this one automatically check, lift, level ballast, and refasten lines.

Arch bridges

On an arch bridge, the arch can be above or below the track. In the case of the world's largest steel-span arch bridge, stretching 1,650 ft (503 m) over the harbor at Sydney, Australia, it is above it. The Pfaffenberg Zwenberg Bridge in Austria is the longest concrete-span arch bridge, at 660 ft (200 m).

Cantilever bridges

The longest cantilever span in the world is the Quebec Bridge in Canada. It opened in 1917 and carries the track of the Canadian National Railway over the St. Lawrence River. The most famous is the Forth Bridge near Edinburgh in Scotland. This was built by 4,500 workers and took seven years to complete.

The Forth Bridge is 8,298 ft (2,529 m) long and crosses the Firth of Forth at a height of 156 ft (47.5 m).

Girder bridges

Girder bridges are usually used to span narrow gaps, but sections can be linked to each other. When properly made, they are very strong. For this reason, after the collapse of the Tay Bridge (in 1879), the new designer, W.H. Barlow, decided to use a series of girder bridges.

Sturdy upright pillars support the metal girders that carry the track.

55

MOVING GOODS

Railroad companies earn most of their money by carrying goods from place to place. In some places, such as Russia, this side of rail transport is vital. However, moving goods from factories to customers, from ports to inland destinations, is a complicated business to organize. All over the world, railroads have built special areas called marshalling yards where goods are sorted. Maschen yard near Hamburg, Germany, is probably the most modern marshalling yard in Europe. In a single day, it can handle 120 southbound trains as well as 150 going north. There are 190 miles (306 km) of track packed into 690 acres (283 hectares) at Maschen. Yet very few people operate the yard, because computers do most of the work.

A modern marshalling yard

Marshalling yards must be efficient. Journey times have to be speedy and trains must be organized as quickly as possible. It is also essential that the right goods reach the right destination. Marshalling yards are usually divided into two sections. In one, wagons gather as trains enter the yard. In the other, long trains bound for the same destination are put together.

A signal box

In both marshalling yards and on the main line, accidents must be avoided and trains moved by switches onto the correct routes. The first signalmen did this work in signal boxes. They moved levers that controlled wires that in turn worked the signal arms and the switches on the line. Messages were sent from station to station by means of electric bells and by Morse Code signals tapped out on telegraph lines. By the 1890s, signals and switches were connected and could be operated together.

Freight
A long line of heavily laden freight cars may need power units in the middle and at the rear, as well as the unit at the front. The crew in the front unit operate the others by remote control.

The control tower
This is the center of operations in the marshalling yard. In a large yard, the work is mainly done by computer. The computer gathers information from incoming trains in advance of their arrival and plans where they need to be directed.

Control
When goods come into some marshalling yards, diesel shunting engines push the wagons over a hump. The hump slows the wagons and allows them to be rolled downhill into the correct area of the yard to join their train.

The hump

Signaling

Methods of signaling have altered greatly over the last 150 years. Men with flags were replaced by various systems of mechanical arms, or "semaphore." These were operated by wires from signal boxes and had colored lamps fitted for night use. Today, colored lights control particular sections of tracks or "blocks" into which a railroad is divided. The green light indicates the block ahead is clear.

A semaphore "Stop" signal

The red light indicates "Stop"

Sidings

The wagons that make up outgoing trains are sent to the correct siding by the computer at the hump. The railroad workers uncouple the wagons as they roll in. Standard-sized containers (page 45) are usually moved on and off flatcars by crane.

Retarders on the track slow speeding wagons.

Turntables

Turntables are made from sections of track that can be swung around in a circle. It is essential to have these at the end of lines to turn steam or diesel locomotives around so that they do not have to make their return journey backward. The world's largest turntables are 135 ft (41 m) and were developed to take the giant *Big Boy* locomotives (page 37).

New methods

Many railroads try to reduce the need for marshalling yards. It is sometimes possible for business customers to make up whole trains of their own goods in private sidings. Locomotives then haul these trains directly to their destinations.

GOING FOR A RIDE

Railroads are used to attract your attention. Famous engines decorate postage stamps; railroad scenes from the past are often used in film and television programs. Composers have even written pieces of music inspired by railroads.

Some people are so enthusiastic about railroads that they are prepared to give up their spare time to repair and rebuild old train engines. One of the most unusual of these "trains for fun" takes its passengers back into the times of the Old West, with men dressed up as bandits carrying out raids on the trains. Many countries now have huge railroad museums such as the German Museum at Mulhouse, and the Indian Rail Transport Museum in New Delhi.

Pleasure travel
People travel by train often for no other reason than the simple pleasure of the trip. In fairgrounds and theme parks all over the world, rollercoaster cars twist and turn, climb and dip, rush through water, and even loop-the-loop.

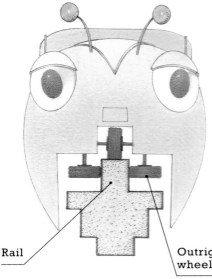

Rail

Outrigger wheels

Monorails
The ladybug train runs on a single rail or "monorail." There are different kinds of monorails; this one follows what is called the "Alweg" system. On either side of the rail is a narrow roadway. The train has wheels that run on the rail, and balancing outrigger wheels. The Alweg monorail in India, the Patiala Railway, is around 60 miles (96 km) long.

Early days
In 1810, the first known monorail opened to carry food for troops in London, England. It was built with wooden boards nailed to posts, and horses pulled the cars. In 1876, General Roy Stone built the first monorail to carry passengers across Fairmont Park in Philadelphia, Pennsylvania.

The outrigger wheels run along the roadway on each side of the rail and hold the train steady.

In miniature

Steam locomotives made such an impact that toymakers began making models of them in tin and wood. Early steam-driven engines left trails of water behind and are therefore usually called "dribblers." Clockwork motors were used, too. The German firm Marklin led the way in developing standard engines. In Britain, in 1920, Frank Hornby began to produce train sets that rivaled the fine ranges made by Marklin.

Today, making and running model trains is a very popular hobby.

Other monorails

The Alweg system is one of three main types. The Lartigue method balances the train over the rail as on the Irish Line (page 29). The Langen type is still in use in Germany, taking people over the Wupper River in cars that hang below a single rail.

Record breakers

Which is the world's smallest public railroad? There are a number of contenders for this title. This is the Romney, Hythe, and Dymchurch line in southeast England. It opened in 1927 and runs on 15 in (380 mm) gauge track. The line from Wells Harbor in England has track only 10 in (260 mm) wide.

59

AT TOP SPEED

People have always enjoyed going as fast as possible in whatever type of transportation is available. Most business executives like to spend as little time traveling as possible. Modern highways and airlines are threats to passenger rail travel, but many of the world's railroads have rallied by providing very fast, quiet, and comfortable trains. In 1991 in Germany, for example, a new service of high-speed, gleaming white trains began a service between the cities of Hamburg and Munich at speeds that reach 175 mph (282 kph). Like most new high-speed sources, this one is powered by electricity. Pantographs link the overhead power line to the locomotive.

Staying on the rails
High-speed trains need special track. When Japanese Railways developed their high-speed trains, they laid standard gauge track. When the trains joined 3 ft 6 in (1,066 mm) track, a third rail had to be added.

Pantograph

125s in Australia
Railroads have played a very important part in the development of Australia. They join together widely separated cities. This XPT service is based on the High Speed 125 diesel-electric locomotives used by British Rail. Like the British version, each 125 has two power cars fitted with twelve-cylinder, turbo-charged diesel engines. Services running at up to 100 mph (160 kph) link the cities of Sydney and Melbourne.

Controlling trains at top speed

The faster trains speed along, the harder it is for the engineer to see the ordinary line-side signals. Very fast trains also take time to slow down and stop. This means, for example, that there are no level crossings on the lines traveled by Japan's bullet trains. Today, the electronics revolution has transformed the problem of controlling high-speed expresses.

Computers are used in many countries to gather, organize, and send out information. They plan the journeys of trains, detect changes that need to be made, and pass on instructions. This is a control center on the high-speed Paris to Lyons route in France. A small number of people control a complicated system by keeping in radio contact with the train crew.

The bullet train
Japan's bullet train pioneered very high-speed services as early as 1965. Gleaming, aerodynamically designed trains hurtled along a route between Tokyo and Osaka at speeds up to 131 mph (210 kph). This *shinkansen* route (page 47) proved enormously popular; on one day in 1975, it carried over 800,000 passengers. By May 1976, more than 1,000 million people had traveled on it.

The TGV
In 1981, SNCF (the French National Railways) launched their new high-speed service of "Trains à Grande Vitesse" (TGV). A special new track had been laid from Paris to Lyons. Along it rushed an express train that reached a new world record speed of 238 mph (380 kph)! Its average speed cut the journey time between the two cities by almost half. The train's very powerful disk brakes bring it to a halt in 1.86 miles (3.1 km).

DOWN THE LINE

In many countries, new railroad lines are being planned and built, and new kinds of locomotives are being developed. At one time, it seemed that air travel might destroy long-distance rail journeys, but new high-speed trains have shown that railroads can compete successfully. Oil has become more expensive, and trains powered by electricity are clean and do less damage to the environment than airplanes and cars.

Some of the new high-speed trains run on specially built new track, but trains have also been developed that can rush at very high speeds over existing track. Engineers are even developing trains, such as the maglev, that will float on magnets.

In the future

All over the world, governments are rethinking and replanning their transportation systems to make trains a central part of travel in the future. Moreover, travel between countries is becoming easier. It is possible to travel greater distances because of the building of new tunnels and bridges and the standardization of gauges.

Monorails

Speedy city travel by train has also been made possible by building above the streets. This monorail system is 8 miles (13 km) long. It opened in Japan in 1964 and links Tokyo to the airport at Haneda. Since these systems do not cause pollution, they offer an attractive form of city travel for the future and several countries are now considering building monorails into and out of cities.

Underground trains

As cities continue to become more crowded, travel by underground trains still presents the speediest way to get around. Modern electronics mean that it is possible to run the latest trains automatically. This is one of the driverless trains that serves the Métro system in the French city of Lille. It runs along quietly on rubber wheels, picking up instructions from the track about the correct speed, and where it should stop and start.

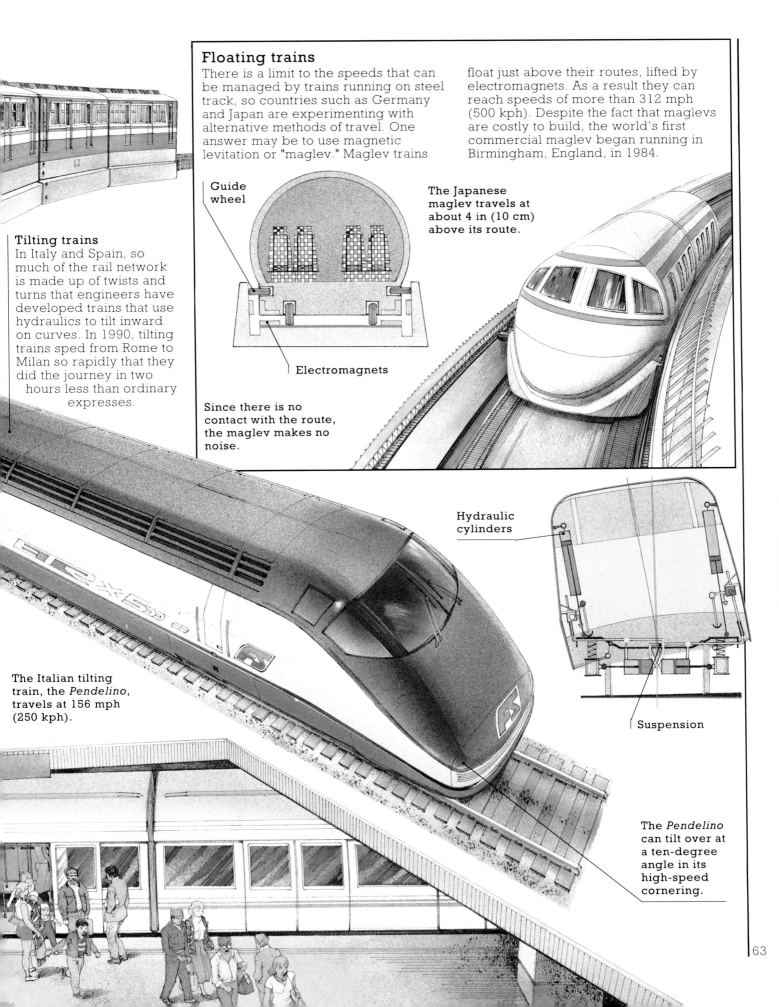

Floating trains

There is a limit to the speeds that can be managed by trains running on steel track, so countries such as Germany and Japan are experimenting with alternative methods of travel. One answer may be to use magnetic levitation or "maglev." Maglev trains float just above their routes, lifted by electromagnets. As a result they can reach speeds of more than 312 mph (500 kph). Despite the fact that maglevs are costly to build, the world's first commercial maglev began running in Birmingham, England, in 1984.

Guide wheel

The Japanese maglev travels at about 4 in (10 cm) above its route.

Electromagnets

Since there is no contact with the route, the maglev makes no noise.

Tilting trains

In Italy and Spain, so much of the rail network is made up of twists and turns that engineers have developed trains that use hydraulics to tilt inward on curves. In 1990, tilting trains sped from Rome to Milan so rapidly that they did the journey in two hours less than ordinary expresses.

The Italian tilting train, the *Pendelino*, travels at 156 mph (250 kph).

Hydraulic cylinders

Suspension

The *Pendelino* can tilt over at a ten-degree angle in its high-speed cornering.

INDEX

Acknowledgements
Dorling Kindersley would like to thank Janet Abbott, Lynn Bresler,
Richard Czapnik, Marcus James, and *Tunnels and Tunnelling*
magazine for their help in producing this book.